The Allegory

The Allegory

Poetic Pursuit of Purpose

E. D. Smith

Dedication

This book is dedicated to my beautiful loving wife. You are my source of inspiration. You are my motivation. I understand that gifts of diamonds and gold are only expressions of the things that one values that cannot be weighed nor measured: love. I will never say you are worth your weight in gold. That is not enough. Love Child Smith, you are worth your weight in love! I absolutely love you.

Table of Contents

Table of Contents

Introduction

Welcome to "The Allegory," Poetic Pursuit of Purpose. There is a rhyme, rhythm, and reason to the journey called life. There's a darkness and illumination, hatred and love, chaos, and peace. One has to acknowledge them all. With all honesty, I can say, "I've experienced them all. And yes because of me, some of you have as well." I look back over my life, not with regrets but as a student. I received the blessing of my lessons. My poetry is how I express the lessons that have been revealed to me by way of life experiences, observations, and conversations. I make no claim that my work is the gospel truth. I do stand behind every word as my truth. Are there any biblical truths within? Absolutely! Will you find contradictions, challenging, or offensive statements? Maybe. I feel that is a beautiful thing. If I can invoke spiritual thought and conversation, then I've done my job. The ability to rationalize and reason is what separates us from being primates. It is that

God in you that raises the guard in you to protect your spiritual intellect. Let us use said intellect to view spiritual things from a new, not better, but different perspective, so that we may all come to a common understanding of the gospel. Surely, we will not see everything in the same light. My thoughts are not your thoughts because my life experiences are not your life experiences. I hope that you will come to find some part of my work to resonate in your spirit. I must admit that my work is an acquired taste and can be considered bitter to some. I advise you to take small manageable bites, savor and enjoy.

Judas

Who is Judas? You'd say, "The disciple that betrayed our Lord and Savior Jesus Christ." Who is Judas? You'd say, "The disciple who received thirty pieces of silver, was overcome with remorse and took his own life." Who is Judas? It would seem I don't know. I've answered the question twice. Your answer is void of revelation and no true perspective. It is bias, judgmental, and nonobjective. Allow me to enlighten your spirit and elevate your mind. Upon reading the scriptures, you will find that the story of Judas was written before the beginning of time; keep this in mind. We have the Son of God, innocent, yet willing to be a slave. Born of a virgin but destined for the grave. Catalyst: Judas. We have the Son of Man. When baptized, the Holy Spirit descended like a dove. Because of the Father's love, He was sent to shed His blood. The effects of Judas. We have the Bright and Morning Star fasting for forty days, in the fourth watch, He prayed. We have the audacity to question the choices He made concerning Judas. Jesus knew exactly who Judas was and still chose him. He knew exactly what Judas had planned and didn't expose him. In fact, that night Jesus washed Judas's feet, gave him wine to drink, and bread to eat. Judas partook in the first sacrament that night because Christ understood that betrayal was his purpose in life. If not Judas, then who would fulfill the prophecy? If not Judas, then who would push Jesus to His cross? If Judas was not obedient to his flesh, there would be no salvation and the world would be lost. Saints, I beseech you to look at your life today. Someone in your past called you nothing and emotionally threw you away. Who was the supervisor that antagonized you? They inspired you to become successfully self-employed. It was the Judas in them that gave you testimony and a reason to Praise the Lord. Yokes are destroyed through salvation. Let's be for real. We don't choose it without confrontation and extreme desperation. So, despise not your enemies or those who did you wrong. If it had not been for their Judas effect, you wouldn't have known you were that strong. There is one more revelation I'd like to give to you. When Jesus prayed, "Father forgive them for they know not what they do…" I believe in my heart of heart He was praying for Judas too.

Reflections

The Cross

At the cross, where I first saw the light and the burdens of my heart rolled away. It was there by faith I received my sight. Allow me to ask a few questions if I may. If you needed something to live and I had it to give, would you receive it? If I told you this gift from me is absolutely free, would you believe it? More importantly, who would you project and direct your gratitude toward? Are you addressing the cross or the one on the cross, when you say thank You Lord? You see, we've been taught to view the cross as the symbol of our salvation. That in reality is only an execution or demonstration of an intimate conversation. Please, walk with me through the garden of Gethsemane. Way before the persecution and strife, He laid down His life, and all the beatings he endured. When He digressed and said nevertheless, that's where our salvation was assured. Think not that I've come against the cross. It is a lighthouse, a safe harbor for the lost. But there is a grave concern.

When they come to the cross and our paths cross, what will they learn? Are we crossed; bitter and hateful or are we crossed; submitted and grateful? As children of the Most High, even if our life is the cost; our conversation and walk should point at the cross. So, if you're named the name, let it be the purpose you pursue. People are not saved because you wear a cross, but because the cross wears you. At the Cross.

Reflections

Where is the Love

What would you say is the true passion of Christ? Is it A. Condemnation, annihilation, and strife? Or is it B. The presentation and preservation of life? I know we all would do the Churchy thing and choose option B. The real question that needs to be asked, would our actions agree? What happened to the love that Christ spoke of when He commanded Peter to feed His sheep? We went from; my powers engage for this present age; I have a charge to keep. Now it's, I pay my tithes so I can reside in a house I cannot afford. It's my fancy car and I'm a superstar, it is the evidence of my covenant with the Lord. Where is the love? If I was a known liar and I told you the truth, would you believe me? If I was profound and profane at the same time, would you receive me? If the truth is the truth, does it matter about the presentation? I know it's not right to judge people for their past, what about their present situation? Where is the love? What's the difference between choices and decisions? What's the difference between spirituality and religion? Which one is worse, sin or transgression? Which one is better, atonement or confession? Where is the love? I can ask a thousand questions and get a thousand answers or a thousand suggestions. We sow three percent tithes and expect a thousand-fold blessing. I can go to a hundred different churches with a hundred different denominations. I can read a hundred different Bibles with a hundred different translations. There are fifty teachers and fifty preaches that are more than willing to say that the other forty-nine are wrong. Now, we'll say the teachers are dry and dull with no fire, and the preachers hoop and holla for too long. Where is the love? Love is Agape, to just call it godly is only describing its source. It's ascribing value to something and holding yourself accountable, without the option of choice. Think! For God so loved the world, even before the earth, moon, or the mighty rushing winds. He sacrificed His only begotten Son for the remission of our sins. So, I will show Him that I love Him and rededicate my life. Because He told me that He loves me when He showed me that I was worth Christ. There is the love.

Reflections

Supposed to Be

Suppose I propose an objective perspective of probability. That is a different way to say, I'm not where I'm supposed to be. Supposedly! You think somehow; a decision based upon lifestyle and religion put you in the position you're in right now. How? So, when facing adversity, should you have kept your cool? When attending that university, should you have stayed in school? Your life would be much better if you hadn't broken that rule. But wait, what about destiny and fate? What about the reality you had the opportunity to create? If you were supposed to be, then that means it's too late. What about restoration and reconciliation? Think before you take future probabilities out of the equation. It's really about being open and objective. You must see the big picture with clarity of perspective. Stand in your right now moment with no regrets, judging everything you've done. You were immature and young. You made every decision and now you're living in the outcome. You can say I could've been, or you can say I shall be. Reject all regrets and receive every opportunity. Learn from your past mistakes, not just what to and not to do. Know that every decision you make will create your world for you. Your present is the product of your immature powerful past. Your future has the potential for promised purpose. You need only to ask.

Reflections

Blame

Listen oh, ye beautiful nation. Allow me to lay truth as our foundation. Those whom we charge for our unfortunate situations are needed to facilitate our vindication. So, if we are truly seeking exoneration, let's be mindful of our delegation. You were healed by whose stripes? By whose name do you decree? Who is the way, truth, and the life? Who walked on water and was the power to part the sea? If you proclaimed His name and named the name of Christ, do you really believe your salvation is trumped by your vice? How can the devil control your life? Think about how we overreact. Every time something doesn't go our way, what's the first thing we say? It's a demonic attack. All that the devil stole, he got to give it back. The scriptures are true, that statement is a fact. If he stole it, he owes, but what if our life is off track? It's our Father's loving rebuke that brings us all back. How do you respond to a wayward child who is covered by the blood? You give them exactly what they are asking for. You know, chasten the ones you love. Your strife is your strife. Your vice is your vice. Help me to understand how you give credit to the devil and man for God's hand and plan designed for your life. So, if all things work for the good of those that Love the Lord; who gets the glory if you're not utterly destroyed? Unfortunately, when your devil has your face, the spirit of chastisement is on your case. The only blessing you get is mercy and grace. The Father will not make you comfortable in your disobedient place. Come from among them. We are called by His name. Let the redeemed of the Lord say, "Father, help me, it's me, and I take the blame."

Reflections

By His Stripes

I am healed from the physical and emotional pains of my past. I receive the joy of Him who healed me and His peace that will forever last. I am healed from unforgiveness because I choose to forgive. He sat before me life and death and I choose to live. I am healed, in my mind, body, and soul. I am covered in His blood which has made me whole. I am healed from illegal soul ties and parasitic relationships. I am in Godly covenants that strengthen and nurture my gifts. I am healed, and for that, I owe my gifts and my life. I give them freely because I was healed by His stripes.

Reflections

I am His Nation

How can a house stand without truth as its foundation? Women give birth to children; men give birth to nations. I am bound by this truth. I'm the god of this earth. Marked for greatness at conception, marked for death at birth.

Born into a world with everything against me. Life comes with strife and pain and his aim is to convince me. Poverty, prison, and death are my portions. If I'm dead to my purpose, then I'm a walking abortion. Born into my first death at my first birth. Being raised into a house of sin is not generational; it's an ancestral curse. But there is something on the inside that I just can't explain. When I settle in this dark place, He keeps calling my name. I trudge toward His voice. There is peace in this place. I feel the warmth of His embrace and I seek His face. When His love overtakes me, I don't know what to do. I'm unclean with the filth of my past and you want me to receive you? He cleaned me and healed me, MAN THIS

IS CRAZY! My confession to this world, Jesus saved me. He gave me His love, grace, mercy, and patience. It was all done for me because I am His Nation.

Reflections

Lost and Found

Father, it is me, your humble servant, and the superstar. Isn't it funny how the lack of money causes you to remind God of who you are? Let's not go too far. Backup, reflect, do you recall? After all, He created, orchestrated, and designed us all. Your issues are small compared to God's vision. While the earth travels, we see hell as reaping from our bad decisions. It's not about religion. Are you a Christian, Catholic, Muslim, or Jew? Even if you are Hebrew, the dominion of earth was given at birth. If it has no worth the blame is on all of you. We read, believe, even bleed because our doctrine is true. Well, can you perceive and conceive the principles presented to you? In the purest form, what does it tell you to do? Think! With love and kindness have I drown all men? With our foolish pride and prejudice, we reject because of your sin. But then again, we're just men. That excuse is the lamest of the lame. There's a famine in the land, yet we seek fortune and fame. I'll rest in mammon's hand as long as the world knows my name. We're called to feed the hungry and heal the lame. We won't do it if there's nothing to gain. So, listen up all you boys and girls. I'm talking Priest, Prince, Dukes, and Earls. We don't lose our souls for gaining the world. The ones that are lost are those who choose to remain in the world.

Reflections

l am Amen

In the beginning, before our path to perdition was paved with religious traditions. Out of triple darkness, there came a petition. Let us create man and let him subdue? I have a question I'd like to propose to you. It's not who was talking and to whom were they talking to? It's; do you realize they were talking about you? You are made in the image and likeness, a reflection. When He said it is good; what He was seeing in you, perfection. Out of His imagination, you were born. Out of the dust of stars, you were formed. With His divine intellect, you were adorned. When you stepped out of His will, you were scorned. Let's fast forward to the present day, it doesn't matter what you do, think, or say, our Father will see you in the exact same way. You are still a child of the Most High. I'm talking more than a mere twenty-two X's and one Y. You are a man. Don't let gender block you from His truth. Before you were formed in the womb, He knew you. Therefore, before you ignore your potential, promise, and purpose of your life, let's restore your joy from the wilds of strife and the bonds of your vice. You are a man. When your soul says yes to God's plan, you'll find rest in God's hand. You are a man, on one accord with the Lord. Health and wealth are restored. Yokes are destroyed. You are a man. It can't just be a decree. Your actions must agree. I'm talking about, it is so, it is written, and so mote it be. You are a man. There's another revolution I need you to see. You end every prayer with amen, which means you agree. Our heavenly father has been called I am, listen carefully. Please understand and comprehend what you are saying. Now repeat after me. I AM A MAN!!!

Reflections

For I Reckon

For I reckon; I'll perpetually participate in worship and praise. I'll get my portion of promise because a good hallelujah; pays. Push, pause because that is a problem. Perhaps, putting our Protagonist at the point will solve them. Why do people mistakenly perceive purpose and potential? Knowing who you're called vs. what they say you can be is very essential. For I reckon, attention in Bible study, you did not pay. He said I am the life, the truth, and the way. Yes, there is power in His blood and name, but what did He say? Seek ye first the kingdom and the promises added to you, He will. If seeking the kingdom teaches us how to abundantly live, why are salvation participants playing let's make a deal? The devil is a patient predator, he's for real. He positions his pawns to take advantage of our propensity to act on how we feel. Perhaps, it's the lack of patience in this right now generation. We are episodes, living demonstrations. Prophets called to prophesy over nations. We're using our power to pray over personal situations. Please people, put love back into the equation. Let your passion for promise be proportioned to your pursuit of purpose and believe that every word of God is true. And when you do; Deuteronomy said promises will pursue and overtake you.

Reflections

The Seek

Write the vision and make it plain. I want wealth, health, fortune, and fame. I want a big car, a big house, and the world to know my name. These are my requests or decrees; it depends on who I'm talking to. I'm depending on the Lord to open the doors I plan on walking through. Father, now that I have a chance; I thank you in advance for what you are about to do. Pause! This is a reenactment of a misinterpretation of Habakkuk's second chapter, verse two. Habakkuk's second chapter, verse one mandates you to write down what He says to you. Are you a prophet to the nations? Are you seeking signs, wonders, and seasons? Your ears are pressed to His lips for what reason: for the next generation or is it self-pleasing? I refuse to believe you knowingly or willingly deceive yourself. Someone planted a seed with malice intent to deceive that you continue to foolishly accept. Now, if it is true that Jesus spoke of you in Matthew chapter 6 verse 32, let's just say the fault is not on you, what shall you do? Pause!!! There's absolutely nothing wrong with desiring the finer things in life. It's when they turn into a vice and begin to replace Christ.. You know; accolades and being wealthy becomes a healthy indication of salvation. What you call having good relations is when you can take good vacations. So, let your vision board be thus saith the Lord. Acknowledge Him in all you do. Jesus is the truth, telling the truth and He will adore you. That's why He died for you. It is only when seeking the kingdom first through Christ; these things become true. All of your desires and more will be added to you.

Reflections

Successful

Success is not measured by suffixes, prefixes, and titles that surround your name. Success is not measured by medals, plaques, and honors for being the best player in the game. Success is measured by the inheritance you leave for your children's children to be a Godly influence throughout your family tree. Success is measured by your family living within God's standards, having a kingdom impact on their community. Success is generational, so set God as your foundation. The true measure of success is when you're being blessed and have a Godly impact on all the nations.

Reflections

Suffer the Little Children

Suffer little children and forbid them not to come unto me. Not allowing them to suffer in the process is our responsibility. The children are the inheritance of the Lord, placed under our care. We should be patient, loving, and forgiving, more importantly always be there; to correct them when they stray, catch them when they fall, comfort them when they fear, and listen when they call. Our presence is worth more than silver and gold. It is the impartation that sets the foundation in which they stand when they grow old. Their purpose is not our decision; it's the Most High. Our purpose is stability and provision, and we must try to understand the foundational truth; the fact that our youth are being destroyed. Let us teach them that their minds and their time should be invested in the Lord. You see, it is our conduct and character that frame the world in which they grow. Suffer the little children and train them in the way they should go. We teach education, good job, or go pro;

instead of having a relationship with a good God and how to sow. Suffer the little children; forbid them not to come unto me. We can learn a lot about our lives through their eyes because they only reflect what they see.

Reflections

Perfection

I am a perfect man. Purposed through all my imperfections. I'm a purposed man, through Christ there is no rejection. He said, forgive you seven times seventy. Does that mean seven times seventy is the number of times he's willing to forgive me? In my transparency, I think I'm close to my four hundred and ninety for sure, but he said I can do exceedingly above all you can hope for. He knew I was going to do what I did when the opportunity presented itself. If there's no condemnation, I offer no explanation, nor justification, so I won't waste my breath. I understand, I'm just a man with a million opportunities to fail. I will prevail as long as I don't dwell on the promises of heaven or the penalties of hell. The fallacy of my mentality was a travesty. I thought the world revolves around me. Even a blind man can see that has nothing to do with ministry. Stop being a tool and be an instrument, a vessel filled with purpose promised to the nation. Christ took care of all salvation; our vocation is reconciliation and restoration. We are living epistles, read of all men. Our story is for His glory. We are saved despite our sin. I am a perfect man. Purposed through all my imperfections. I'm a purposed man, through Christ there is no rejection.

Reflections

Birthright

I realize I'm living in a world of real lies. It's no surprise that I cause my own demise because I can't see with my real eyes. As a matter of fact, scratch that. The world is not what I need to be looking at because I view the world how my own ideology projects. In retrospect, it's really cause and effect. Whatever I think in my heart, so shall I be. Translation: I allowed the world to influence and lie to me. Disease, death, and poverty is now part of my reality. Question? Is it not written; I am a child of the Most High? Then, tell me why I receive information designed to deceive and now I believe that lie? I was never supposed to be sick nor poor and never supposed to die. How do you subdue the most powerful being on this Earth? You make me believe I have no worth. You convince me to receive the information that I was born to be cursed. You make me see and say that one day I'll ride in a hearse. Whatever a man thinketh in his heart is the construct of his reality. The world took my power, purpose, and promise and used it against me. You see; wisdom and intellect are your first true light. The imagery of your imagination is your first true sight. Immortality: in reality, is your birthright.

Reflections

Imagine

Imagine you are walking into your favorite convenient store. You can hear the bell as you walk through the door. There is a display of 12 packs in the middle of the floor. Imagine you notice a young lady at the counter buying cigarettes and playing the lotto. Her race is not important; we'll just say mulatto. She's medium built, kind of slim. She is wearing a fitted black T-shirt with the words 'praise Him'.

Imagine behind that thick glass is a clerk whose body language is saying hurry up and make a decision. With a smirk on his face, he says, "I'm glad I'm not a part of your religion."

Pause! How do you approach this situation? Now, you represent the church, so no confrontation and no condemnation.

Do you:
A: Stand silently in the background and judge in fear? Do you have the right to fight? You're buying condoms and beer.

B: Do you protect her in love with mercy and grace? Will you check that clerk and wipe that smirk off his face?

Imagine it's the same store, the same situation, the exact same day. When the guy in the fitted black T-shirt turns around and thanks you for protecting him, do you feel the same way?

Pause! It is not real. The ebb and flow of your emotion are based on a hypothetical situation. Let's lay truth as our foundation. The truth is, as long as Christ lives there will be no condemnation. Not for the hypocritical you nor that young man that we all call lost. Christ died on the cross, He paid the cost. Now, let us have a moment of clarity and address the real issue at hand. Focus on revelation and not how you responded to that young man.

Truth: You literally heard that bell when you walked through that door. You gave a brand name to those 12 packs in the middle of the floor. Until I said condoms and beer, you didn't know why you were in the store. We are all blessed with vivid imaginations. Apparently, yours work just fine. As you process this revelation, please keep one thing in mind.

There is absolutely no truth in thinking or speaking you don't or can't see or imagine you being whatever God has called you to be.

Reflections

God's Plan

My plans are my plans. My will is my will. You're in my hands. Desire what you will. I will pay the bill. I am Jehovah-Nissi. I will dispel the plans of your enemy. From sickness, disease, to lack and poverty. It is my pleasure and divinity that you have health, wealth, and prosperity. I will bless your house. For you have made it a home. You are never alone. I will multiply the harvest from the seeds you've sewn. I'm not a man that I should lie. Every word I say is true. Hope and prosperity are the plans I have for you.

Jeremiah 29:11

11 For I know the thoughts that I think toward you, saith the Lord, thoughts of peace, and not of evil, to give you an expected end.

Reflections

I am Here

In your darkest hour when it seems all hope is lost. I am here to remind you that I paid the cost. You can cry if you want to, mourn if you want to; I will never leave nor will I ever forsake you. I know life has a way of ruining your day. The winds will come to blow you away. The rains will come to flood you with pain. When you're at the lowest of lows just call my name, and I'll trade my joy and peace for your sadness and sorrow. This is the day I've made, and I'll give you a brighter tomorrow. I am here for you; to see through life's ups and downs. You were never alone nor on your own; I am always around. So, when you walk through life in the midst of strife be bold and have no fear. Because you're my child, I'll bring you a smile and remember I am always here.

Reflections

He Is

ut without faith, it is impossible to please Him: for he that cometh to God must believe that He is...

The one Lord that I submit to His ways: my Adonai.

The true and living God whom I worship and praise, my Jehovah-Elohim.

The one I turn to when I'm afflicted with pain and disease; my Jehovah-Rapha.

The holder of the peace to put my soul and mind at ease; my Jehovah- Shalom.

The provider and sustainer of all my needs; my Jehovah-Jireh.

The standard, my banner; my enemies take heed; my Jehovah-Nissi.

The good shepherd, my protector; I am never alone; my Jehovah-Rohi.

The giver of righteousness and mercy and grace to atone; my Jehovah-Tsidkenu

and that He is a rewarder of them that diligently seek him.

Reflections

Love

Love is the most powerful thing in existence. Despite time or distance, Love is eternally consistent. Love is a principal thing. It's foundational. Love is steadfast and sometimes confrontational. It can be defined as undefinable. Love is whatever you need plus all of the above. You can't quantify the magnitude of its majesty. With a primitive understanding, we say, "God is Love." Now, the earth is the LORD's, and the fullness thereof. As the body of Christ, I suffice, we are that selfsame Love. This revolution should bring clarity of perspective to the collective. It's called unity. The body is a community. When I love and forgive you; in reality, I love and forgive me. Love gave His Son for the salvation of humanity. Do we have a kingdom mentality when it comes to our ministry? Are we using our gifts for selfish prosperity or feeding the hungry and building our community? Let's dispel the spell of a false religious identity. For God so loved the world, not just humanity. We've not come against prosperity. It just can't be the rule. It's only a tool to ensure the gospel is a reality. One day, we will be called to glory. The children are going to read our life story. Be careful how we ministry today. For tomorrow it shall be our allegory.

Reflections

Allegory

Come let us bear witness to the Lord's light. Let's use sound right reasoning. But for some reason; something doesn't sound right. All your hell wasn't even about you. It doesn't matter what you say or do. That life was ordained for you when you were broke, broken, and left for dead. God called you His son and anointed your head. You see, the distance between you and salvation is perspective. Learn to see you how He sees you. Be objective. What you call hell, and a hot mess is only a press so that you can express the real you. Whatever you did or didn't do. All the so-called bad times you've gone through. There's one consistent thing that rings true. It didn't kill you. You may have been battered and beaten but never destroyed. Now, you have a testimony about the goodness of the Lord. Go and testify to the next generation. They benefit from your current situation. Don't be ashamed of your story. With revelation your epistle shifts from being a mere testimony to the wisdom of an allegory.

Reflections

Shift

A Shift is the realization that your spiritual confrontation is only an indication that something has changed. We can't see past our own identification with the association of a mode of transportation that denotes acceleration, elevation, or gain. Then why so much pain? Let me explain. Our enemies could care less about the affirmations we confess or our high expectations, declarations, and participation in the weekly alter calls. A shift functions on three different levels. Saints, we must comprehend them all. Come let us walk through the word of The Most High and see what thus saith the Lord. If we can believe and receive the scriptures we read, then the yoke of ignorance will be destroyed.

Level 1: Luke 12:34 is a scripture we love to quote when it's time to give. Let's look at it from a different perspective and apply it to how we live. Our treasures are not diamonds and gold as you would suppose but our values rooted deep down in our core. When questioned it's something we would lie for. It is also paternal and maternal, something we are willing to kill or die for. Now, the heart is our true center, not the organ that resides in our chest. But I digress, you love me is what your lips confess, but your heart is a piping hot mess. Matthews 15:8 is where Jesus said it best. Back to the matter at hand, what really matters is if a man has the ability to understand that a shift has to begin from a heart without sin. David said it best in Psalms 51:10. But of course, here's that voice again telling us we were born in sin. It just can't be done. Who is a liar and a thief, the devil, or Jesus in Matthew 6:19-21? Let us avoid that trap and recap a few scriptures we love to recite. Psalm 19:14 "May the words of my mouth and the meditation of my heart be pleasing in your sight…" Psalm 119:11 I have hidden your word in my heart that I might not sin against thee. Guard thy heart with all diligence; in part, that's Proverbs 4:23.

Level 2: When we read Proverbs 23:7, we have a tendency to omit the most pivotal part. My thoughts and meditation are only a manifestation of the desire that flows from my heart. All of my affirmations and declarations will never reflect in my life until the transformation of my thoughts and mediations in Romans 12:2 are facilitated by Christ.

Level 3: Yes! You will have what you say. That's what the preacher man said. He was misguided now he's misguiding and a whole generation is misled. Brothers and sisters, please get this revelation; the power of life and death is in your declaration, just add a little faith to your convocation. Now, if you're self-centered speak to your situation, but if your heart has been purified through salvation, then to go the highest mountain and prophesy to nations.

Reflections

I Command Thee

Oh, day I command thee. Renew thyself and kneel before me. Make straight my way as I journey through thee. For I am the son of I Am; and when I decree, you must obey because greater is He that is in me.

Oh, life unhand me. For, He came that I might abundantly have thee. I will do His will and you cannot stop me. I am called by His name and I have His authority. You will not prosper with any weapon you've formed against me.

Oh, angels, I charge thee, to bring me my gifts and His word to the natural from the heavenly. As you protect and minister to me, bring revelation in the places I cannot see. Give all that is required of me that I may give birth to a generation that can have dominion and subdue the earth. I acknowledge Him in every way. And with kingdom authority, I command this day.

Reflections

The Apex Predator

Yea, do I walk through the valley of the shadow of death; evil shall fear me. For I am the son of I am and greater is he that is within me. I decree I am a man of God, apex predator, top of the food chain. I submit only to God and the earth, in its fullness is my domain. I believe when I read; I'm above only, that's the apex. I receive when I read not forsaken and never lonely, that's the apex. Yes... I am a worshiper and I praise. Critical thinker as well. How can a weapon prevail? I'm Samson; I'll snatch the gates off of hell. I am an apex predator. Don't mistake my meekness for weakness. It's faith. There's a thorn in my side, I'm void of pride. I am perfect in purpose through grace. I am a man; formed in the image and likeness of the Holy Trinity. I am a predator; a seed of Eve and his seed there is enmity. I am a man, who accepted Christ, salvation, and my immortality. I am a predator; no longer in flesh, my humanity is now my divinity. Yea, do I run through the dark valleys by faith; I don't need to see. I am in the body of Christ with whom you will kneel if you dare to oppose me.

Reflections

Let Me Breath

Here I stand as a black man, olive branch in hand. If you think it is a request, then you don't understand. It's not even a command nor demand. I'm just living according to God's plan. While you're spending your days thinking of ways to make me suffer. There's one who is proficient at prayer and praise; and I'm just a buffer. I am the distance between your desired destiny or death and destruction, either is your fault. You planned my demise but didn't realize that a black woman's prayers are fervent by default. When I leave the house, you best believe my spouse is praying for me. See, my sisters and daughters, they adore me. When I lost my way and didn't know what to say; my grandma and momma prayed for me. If you still need convincing after all I've said, remember, Samson killed thousands of men and a woman cut his dreads. John the Baptist was loved by Christ; a woman made him lose his head. It is in your best interest to let me breathe and to let me be. Before praying on you is the way she prays for me. Let me breathe!

Reflections

Still a Sinner

Didn't I prophesy in Your name? Didn't I testify about my pain? Didn't I give You credit for my gain? Then, why am I still called a sinner? Am I not the bishop, the apostle, and prophet so and so? It's not the ten-thousand-dollar honorarium; it is for You I go. Does not my ministry employ armor-bearers, adjutant, and security on my staff? Don't I minister to the needs and receive the seeds from the sower on Your behalf? Then, why am I still called a sinner? Am I a crook to sell my book and CD in your vestibule? Is the devil upset at my private jet that I use to minister for You? Don't I open every speech and sermon I preach giving honor and glory to You? I need a "come rest my son, job well done," for all the work I do. Father, I ask, why am I still a sinner? My son, it is not My will that My house be filled with My children which remain to be lost. Prophesying in My name got you the gain and you've yet to pick up your cross. Your lips say that you love Me. Your heart craves the admiration of men. The reason I'm not pleased is not the books and CDs, vanity is the root of your sin. You want My stuff for your story. You use My name for your glory. After all, you've done, you're still My son I love and truly forgive you. When you no longer live a lie, you can truly testify Luke seven: twenty-two.

So, He replied to the messengers, "Go back and report to John what you have seen and heard: The blind receive sight, the lame walk, those who have leprosy are cleansed, the deaf hear, the dead are raised, and the good news is proclaimed to the poor."

Reflections

Well Done

When I made the decision to make provision my top priority, my sowing increased, my harvest released, and it starts with my family tree. I am the Abraham of my generation. I set the standard and dig the wells. By the sweat of my brow, I make this vow, my seed will never see hell. I am the good man; I sustain my sons and daughters' daughters and sons. For they are my treasures, it is my good pleasure to get the well done.

My good character is a reasonable service; my ministry is my charge to keep. My praise is for His edification; my gifts give strength to the weak. I understand it is not my abstaining from the things You told me not to do, I understand when I don't comprehend; it is my faith that pleases You. You see I am a giver, cheerful for giving more than the expected return. You've given me more; peace, love, joy, and salvation I could never earn. Perfection is not the criteria for salvation. It is the reception of His only begotten Son. When I'm called to heaven's door, what I'm looking for; is for You to say job well done

Blessed be the faithful ones. May all your endeavors bode well. Curses unto the deceitful ones; you will lift up your eyes in hell. Please don't think because you don't smoke or drink; that God's favor is secured. For it is those who progress in spite of their mess; they will have their blessings assured. We are not saved just to be saved; through the ministry, we give the lost a chance. If we don't do our Father's will; then how can His kingdom advance? Are we called to be non - gamblers or are we prophets to the nations? Peter cursed and still the church was built upon his revelation. We view salvation as a ticket to heaven, yet it is my works that make me His son. You'll be locked in a cell and cast into hell for your disobedience; there you will be well done.

Reflections

My Child

It is my will that you be inspired to inspire, motivated to motivate. You are made in my image; I've created you to create. I equipped you with everything you needed at birth. I've given you dominion, now rule over and subdue the earth. You are more than a mere conqueror; I am more than a mere king. You are the Lord of the earth and I am the Elohim. You are my child whom I planted in the earth like a tree. When the world sees you, I want them to vicariously see Me.

Reflections

Thank You

I appreciate You! This appreciation will be expressed through my gratitude. Your increased value will reflect through my actions, my conversations, and more importantly in my attitude. So, thank You. Thank You for being my salvation and not summoning 12 legions of angels and bypassing Your cross. Thank You for being my demonstration. I know that if I follow You, I will never get lost. Thank You for being my motivation. For the penalties of my past, You paid the cost. Thank you for being my inspiration. I'm above only. I'm the head. I'm a boss. Thank You. Thank You for nothing. That something I wanted was designed to kill me. Thank You in advance for a chance to see that You were only trying to protect and heal me. Thank You for not allowing me to compromise my identity. I realize that I can't differentiate between real and lies, and because of You, I'm still me. Thank You for chasing me. Thank You for your rebukes and for me being chastised. I realize that without Your grace, mercy, and hedges there were certain situations I wouldn't survive. Thank You. There are a million times a million things I should be grateful for. So, I'll say thank You a million times a million and for good measure, I'll throw in one more. Thank you.

Reflections

Life or Death

Dad, are you busy; can I have a minute of your time? Yeah, let's sit down and talk; what's on your mind? I have a problem with the new kids: Death, karma, and life. I don't like either one of them. I need your advice. Death is bigger than Life plus he likes to fight. Karma is a year older. She repeated the 3rd grade. They made up their own rules for every game we played. We planned to race at recess today. When we went out to play, they kept getting in the way. I didn't want to play with them, but you said to be kind. Life's brother stood with his hand out; like he was the finish line. I ran as fast as I could. I gave out of breath. Then Life cheated, of course, and beat me to death. Son, why are you racing to a place you really don't want to be? Why losing to life makes you come to me? Dad, I don't think that's true. Breakfast, lunch, and dinner, before I eat, I say thank you. When I lay me down to sleep, I say l love you. Really! I supply your every thought, want, and need. And a routine response is all you have for me? You are still young. You have a lot to learn. Keep talking. I don't want you to think I'm not concerned. I studied for my quiz all week. I want to do my best. I got a gold star and Karma got a gold star. But she cheated on her test. Son, that sounds like a little envy and jealousy too. What does Karma's reward have to do with you? If I couldn't play and studied all day, then she should too. Then I suppose that little situation exposed you. That mindset will take you down the wrong path. You don't know who sowed seeds on her behalf. What happens through life or to Karma is not your concern. I sent you down there for one purpose; that is to learn. Well, I learned Life doesn't play fair and Karma is a... Whoa!!! That's as far as it goes! I was about to say, Snitch. She tells everything she knows. Death is a bully. He makes everyone afraid. The last person who fought him got put in a grave. When he came around, I just ran and hid. I would beat Death but I'm just a kid. Okay, baby goat. Remember Jesus did.

Reflections

Reincarnation

2 Corinthians 5:17 "Therefore if any man be in Christ, he is a new creature: old things are passed away; behold, all things are become new."

Can we have a conversation? First, let me set the tone and lay the foundation. Search my heart. There's no confrontation. My aspiration is information. Is Christ the head of your life and you've renounced sin? Is it safe to say you're a Christian? Does that mean you're born again? Is your past full of ups, downs, thick and thins? Have you gained a few pounds and lost a few friends? Do you recall the things you've done and gone through? Can you honestly say; that today, that person is not you? If this is true; what did you do? How did you become you? I'm not asking how you went from embryo to a fully evolved adult. That's genetics; a metamorphic result. You are a whole new person living a whole new life. You're full of drive and ambition, but not moved by old news vice. Was this change in your life facilitated by Christ?

So, is it safe to say, "Your current situation is a real-life demonstration of reincarnation?" This is not a debate but a conversation. I know religion says differently from what was taught you. Let every man be a lie and God be true. I showed you the scripture to support me. Now, show me the one that supports you.

Reflections

Religion

I think therefore I am, a victim of mistaken identity. Even though pleasing, for some reason; you base your theology and mortality upon me. I'm amazed at how I garner worship and praise from free men and slaves. Allow me to show you my ways. This is how I present myself to you. I've been called Christian, Catholic, and sometimes Jew. I'm known by many persuasions and denominations. Protestant, Baptist, Lutheran, to name a few. Before all of them, I was known as a Hebrew. Therein lies the truth. I've long realized that you can't see the lies when I sprinkle in a little truth. Many have lied in pursuit of my gain. Many have died and were prosecuted in my name. Murder, martyr it's all the same. When all hell breaks loose the church gets the blame. When there's revival amongst the youth I get the fame. I know at first; you thought I was called the church. You've yet to know my name. I am your life. I am your truth and your way. You live your life in a way that your God didn't say. From the foods, you eat to the days you met and especially the traditions you keep. To believe in me is really heresy. My origins are a mystery. I've hidden myself in your past then I rewrote your history. If you continue to follow me, that's your free-willed decision. Allow me to introduce myself. My name is Religion. Will you come?

Reflections

Hope

Let's pretend for a moment that every word that Jesus says is true. Seek and ye shall find. Knock and it shall be open unto you. Mary said we need wine and then told the servants, "Do whatever He tells you to do." She rejected his disrespect with an, you may be the son of God, but I'm ma'am. Now, do what I expect of you. Do you want to know why we're not experiencing manifestation through mere declaration? Expectation is the X factor in this algebraic equation. See, faith activation is defined with hope as its foundation. Let's be mindful of how we use it in our everyday conversation. We act as if it means wish, want and need. That's a misinterpretation. So, approach every situation with your inward vibration saying, it is already done. I am already healed. The battle is already won. This is the revelation I got when I read Hebrews chapter 11 verse 1.

Now, faith is the substance of things hoped for, the evidence of things not seen.

Reflections

Deliverance

I'm always in need. So, I declare and decree, and then wait to see if there shall be a manifestation. Then I sow a seed for the exact same need. Then I wait and see if there shall be a confirmation. I was taught to lean not and wait on the Lord. I'm losing patience. In spite of sin, I do it over and over again. I still can't win. My faith has shifted to frustrating. Father, I need a revaluation. Fact: you can only attract things on the level of your vibration. Fact: it is your frequency not the frequency of your prayers and supplication. Truth: the presentation of this information is delivered through deliverance and salvation. When you arrive at this destination, you'll be in two places but one location. You easily get over most people. You no longer respond to certain situations. That designation is soul elevation. In lower degrees, the disease of diseases like poverty and cancer invokes the wrong questions from the right answer. Why are you so sick? What did you do? Why you? Answer: you can't deliver people from the things you haven't gone through. So, go on through what you're going through. God and the devil were talking; Job they were discussing you. Here is your answer, answer my Father trusts you. So, Deliver!

Reflections

The Giver

Someone, please help me to fully comprehend. I think I'm a giver. It's the reasoning I don't really understand. What's more important: the lives I've lived or the life I'm living? Is it the size and value of the gifts or the act of giving? What constitutes a seed: time, money, or deed? Am I sowing to meet a need or am I just trying to succeed? Does the latter indicate greed? Is it okay to expect to collect a harvest from the seed I sow? When I feel you say no, I feel neglected and get really disrespectful. Father you owe! I really don't know why I sow? What is my motivation? Am I dodging these bills, pills, or incarceration? If sowing a seed to meet my need, is that considered a righteous intent? If I volunteer at a charity event; is that time invested or just time spent? It's evident; I'm only a philanthropist when I can't make rent. How do you respond to a stranger in need of love? Is your gift laces with a grudge? Judge not lest ye be judged. God loves a cheerful giver. So, govern your attitude. If a man is hungry, don't give him advice; give him food. If he is cold give him the shirt off your back. The best gift you can ever give is a selfless act. Now, I know I am a giver. The reason I truly understand. I am Christ-like and like Christ my life is given for the salvation of man.

Reflections

E. D. Smith

Knowing

What's the difference between knowing and believing? Belief is pre-planning. Knowing is post achieving. Do you believe most don't want a word from God? They really want vindication for their frustration. Did you know, being in relation, that one word can become an eternal conversation? Do you believe, your prayer closet is not only for petitions, it's a confession booth? But honestly, we have a problem being honest with honesty; Jesus is the truth. Did you know, we want deliverance from the consequences of bad decisions, not its demonic roots? Do you believe, how you give has more value than the gift that is given? Did you know that people don't listen when your words don't line up with how you're living? Did you know that when it comes to ministry, our responsibility is to take the word of God out of fictitious theology, by renewing our mentality and showing it as a viable reality? Do you believe that repentance is a demonstration of salvation?

Did you know that when you are forgiven, suffering and strife is really self-condemnation? Do you believe that fasting is not abstaining from preservatives, sweets, and for seven days not eating meat? Did you know that Jesus consumed nothing for forty days? What we call fasting is how we are supposed to eat. How do know what you believe is real? Knowing is based on experience, belief is how you feel. Now you know.

Reflections

Wiser

Wise men have said, wiser men have done, and the wisest man listened to the wise and became wiser. I've read the books, now I know. I have experienced it, now I can show. I know what I know, and what I don't know I am willing to go and submit to the one who is willing to show all they know. That is how I grow; wiser. I read their word to show myself approved. I allow your word to govern my thoughts, my words, and when I move. I am in Him and He is in me, is that one accord? I submit to His will; my purpose is fulfilled when my actions say Jesus is Lord. Wise men have said, wiser men have done; the wisest man submitted to the wiser and became his son. That is how he became wiser.

Reflections

Dear Heavenly Father,

It's me, the one you vowed to never leave alone. Since You gave me my identity, teach me to use my masculinity to be the strength and stability of my home. Teach me to be a son to my father, a husband to my wife, a father to my children, and to always decree life. Give me the strength of Samson and the passion of Christ. I ask not for the things of this world, for Your word will suffice. Yes, I do desire, the blessings of Abraham. The ones I do not deserve. As for me and my house, including the dog and the mouse, Father, You will be served. So, teach me how to be forgiven. Teach me how to forgive. You came that I might have life, so teach me how to live. Give me Solomon's wisdom and David's praise. What I'm really asking is for you to teach me your ways. Yes, I'm meek but my flesh is weak. How can I be saved? I've gone as far as I can go and done all I know to do. From this moment forward I give it all to You. I need for You to be my source and I'll be Your voice. This is my choice. So,

You plot my course. I'll go where and when You say go. I'll come where and when You say come. I want to be more than just a good and faithful servant. I want to hear, "Well done my son."

In Jesus mighty name I pray for this and more, Amen.

Reflections

My Son,

I hear you earnestly pray consistently. I've constantly beckoned you to come unto Me. Yes, you pray faithfully, but from a distance. Come closer so I can elevate your faith beyond My mere existence. There is a reward for your persistence. I Am your Abba; that's father to the unlearned. I offer salvation. That obligation should be your first concern. Do you believe in Me? Do you take heed and receive every scripture you read? Do you get revelation from every biblical story? Can you believe I'll supply your every need according to My riches in glory? I know your store. I authorized, ordained, and orchestrated every second of your life. Let Me get this right? You came to Me for the happiness and stability of your wife. For the security of your family, you'll gladly lay down your life, my son that is the passion of Christ. Do you love Me and place no one above Me? Then feed My sheep. Live your life according to My purpose. You do have a charge to keep. My grace and mercy will abound when your flesh gets weak. You only ask of Me in part when it's My whole kingdom you should seek. The earth is your inheritance, for you are meek. The confession for the source of your blessings and your faith pleases Me. You are healed, whole, and through salvation, you have procured and secured your immortality. Because I count you righteous, this is a due season for you. I will do exceedingly, abundantly; above all, you can hope, dream, or ask Me to do.

It is done!

Reflections

The Affirmation

Live life on purpose. It's not your environment but your design that dictates your destiny. Deciding to do God's will for your life takes determination, dedication, and discipline. More importantly, you must have a will to do so. Your will is an intangible and immeasurable force that surpasses mere want, need, and desire. It is this force that rules over your environment. Nothing can come to you unless you will it so. As your will govern your life; you govern your will with love. Love is given in measure but cannot be measured. No words can truly describe it. You can only describe its application and attributes. Out of it flows all emotions. Because of love, people are inspired, new ideas are birthed, and a new generation is born to carry on the banner of hope for the world. Love is also the reason kingdoms have and will fall and wars are fought. Love is not to be understood but reverenced. Only with the understanding of these things, I make my affirmation.

The Affirmation:

With the love of God, I love you. Within the love of Christ, I will be loved. Because my design, gifts, and talents are what makes me uniquely me; I will use them for my purpose of glorifying God by loving the world as He does.

Reflections

The Beginning

www.ingramcontent.com/pod-product-compliance
Lightning Source LLC
LaVergne TN
LVHW051349080426
835509LV00020BA/3348